I'm Not Broken

The Power of Prayer, Scripture,
and Interactive Journaling

CHRISTINA DEMARA

I'm Not Broken, *The Power of Prayer, Scripture, and Interactive Journaling*
By **Christina E. DeMara-Kirby**

christinademara.com

Published by DeMara-Kirby & Associates, LLC.
McAllen, Texas 78504
Printed in the United States of America
ISBN: 978-1-947442-01-6

Subject Heading: Christian Life / Christian Counseling

All commentary and scripture references are taken from the public domains, World English Bible, Holy Bible, and King James versions.

Christina DeMara and her affiliate DeMara-Kirby & Associates, LLC. are committed to planting seeds of faith. For public speaking engagements or bulk book orders, please contact us at christinademara.com.

CHRISTINA DEMARA
LIFE • LEARNING • LEADERSHIP

Also Written By

CHRISTINA DEMARA

My Prayer Book

Peace is Mine
The Forgiveness Journal

I'm Not Broken
*The Power of Prayer, Scripture, and
Interactive Journaling*

How God Saved Me
*My Mother's Memoirs on Abuse,
Depression & Overeating*

The I Am Journal
A Soul-Searching Journal for Creative Women of God

Isaiah 43:2
*40 Days of Scriptures, Reflection, and
Journaling for the Lent Season*

Meaningful
Books & Resources

Meaningful Leadership
How to Build Indestructible Relationships with Your Team Members Through Intentionality and Faith

Meaningful Leadership Journal

Meaningful Leadership Prayer Book

Meaningful Teacher Leadership
Reflection, Refinement, and Student Achievement

Meaningful Writing & Self-Publishing
Your Guide to Igniting Your Pen, Faith, Creativity & Entrepreneurship

Early Life Leadership
Books and Resources

Early Life Leadership in Children
101 Strategies to Grow Great Leaders

Early Life Leadership
101 Conversation Starters and Writing Prompts

Early Life Leadership Workbook
101 Strategies to Grow Great Leaders

Early Life Leadership Workbook for Girls
101 Strategies to Grow Great Leaders

Early Life Leadership Kids Journal

Early Life Leadership in the Classroom
Resources, Strategies & Tidbits to Grow Great Leaders

Contents

A Note from the Author 11

10 Intentions for this Book 13

The History of Broken Pottery 15

Pray, Reflect, & Write 17

I'm Not Broken 19

The 20 H's of the Bible *19*

Why Did God Create Women? 21

Hollowness 23

Hollowness: Emotional emptiness or a craving

for something more *23*

Harmful: *Anything that harms you emotionally or physically* *29*

Hopelessness: *Giving up or the belief things cannot improve* *37*

Hostage: *That which holds back and shackles* *45*

Humble: *Modesty and having a humble self-opinion* *51*

Honesty: *Honor and respect for the truth* *57*

Healing: *The natural procedure by which the body and mind repairs* .. *63*

Prayer *65*

Healing Activities *66*

Horizon: *Where problem meets solution* *71*

Pray, Reflect & Write *72*

Harmony: *The blend of peace, friendliness, and a cooperation*

of processes and life norms *75*

Pray, Reflect & Write *76*

Health: *Habits that nourish and encourage physical,*

emotional, and mentally wellness *79*

Heritage: *Practices and traditions passed down
from one generation to the next* 83

    Pray, Reflect & Write 84

Honey: *The small things in life that make life extra sweet* 89

    Count your blessings. 90

Humor: *Even Jesus laughs, for laughing is good for the soul!* 93

Heart: *The inner emotion of love* 97

Honor: *Actions taken to honor God* 101

    Pray, Reflect & Write 102

Hands: *The part of a person's body that displays his
or her God-given crafts* 107

History: *Experience and what is learned from one's life* 111

Harvest: *A season in life when hard work pays off* 115

    The Farmer Sowing Seed 118

Heaven: *The earthly things that bring love and delight* 121

Holy Spirit: *The Spirit of God and Jesus Christ that guides us* 127

    The Cracked Pot Folktale 130

Conclusion 133

    Never Underestimate the Power of Prayer 134

    Reading Log 151

About the Author 159

A Note from the Author

Dear Valued Reader,

As women, we often bear the burden of life on our backs, the same way Jesus carried his cross. We carry problems, a growing, and busy family, aging parents, deceit, broken relationships, seasons of hurt and struggle. How does one deal with life changes? How can spirituality help us cope? When I look back at some of the hardest times of my life, I see I never truly "coped." What I see now is how God loved, guided, provided for, and carried me when I wanted to give up. Do Christians cope differently than people of the world? The purpose of I'm Not Broken, The Power of Prayer, Scripture, and Interactive Journaling is to heal, guide, and revitalize the lives of women.

The overall theme of this interactive book is the crack in the pottery that represent the hurts in life that chips away at our souls and often make us question our faith. I am often asked why I took on the difficult task of writing such an intimate book. I am not a theologian. I am not Mother Teresa. I am not perfect. I am, however, a woman made in God's image, like you. I hope this book brings healing and peace to your life and touches a part of your heart and soul.

With warm wishes and a heart of gratitude,

CHRISTINA DEMARA
LIFE · LEARNING · LEADERSHIP

10 Intentions for this Book

1. To motivate the reader to move closer to the cross

2. To encourage independent Bible reading

3. To encourage self-reflection and self-awareness

4. To encourage community by using this book as a book study

5. To encourage healing of the heart and soul

6. To encourage an open mind and different perspectives on Bible beliefs and Scriptures

7. To journal, write all over it, save it, and reflect at a later time

8. To create a spiritual habit of seeking God, Jesus, and the Holy Spirit

9. To deepen the understanding of God's Word

10. To encourage inner peace

The History of Broken Pottery

HISTORICALLY, POTTERY HAS been used by all civilizations. If we go back in history and look at different civilizations and different eras, we will see how it was used in different ways. Pottery has many purposes, from carrying water to honoring the dead. In the same way that God created and molded us in his image, pottery is created with the love and intentionality of someone's hands. However, pottery is delicate and often chipped or broken. There are different things that break pottery: anger, carelessness, and most common accidents, simple slips of the hands—like most things happen in our lives. Chipped pottery is perceived as lessened, but the ancient art of Kintsugi, or Kintsukuroi, repairs pottery with gold. Once the pottery is repaired with gold, it becomes a beautiful piece of art. It becomes more beautiful for its brokenness and is displayed for its artistic improvement. In relation to our faith, when we go through a season of problems, we often feel broken and shattered, like flawed pottery. We can try to put the pieces back together on our own, or we can surrender with the understanding that nothing is capable of holding us together except God, His Son, and the Holy Spirit. Don't compare your life to others because we all have flaws.

Pray, Reflect, & Write

THE INTERACTIVE PAGES in this book include reflection questions, journal outlines, prayer pages, different places to take notes and draw or sketch. This book creates a personalized experience that will help you obtain peace through connecting with God, Jesus, and the Holy Spirit. The reading and activities hope to encourage you to pray, reflect and write your thoughts and feelings. Feel free to revisit your journaling and reflect or add a symbolic drawing or sketch. You can highlight or used colored pens. Feel free to be creative! This is the time to let go and let God!

I'm Not Broken

THE 20 H'S OF THE BIBLE

As YOU TAKE a step to move toward the cross, please think about your life. Let the Holy Spirit guide you. Answer the questions posed throughout the book solely based on your life, your interpretations, and your spiritual beliefs. There are no right or wrong answers. These activities are intended to help you reflect and create an honest and clear picture of your life.

1. **Hollowness:** *Emotional emptiness or a craving for something more*

2. **Harmful:** *Anything that harms you emotionally or physically*

3. **Hopelessness:** *Giving up or the belief things cannot improve*

4. **Hostage:** *That which holds back and shackles*

5. **Humble:** *Modesty and having a humble self-opinion*

6. **Honesty:** *Honor and respect for the truth*

7. **Healing:** *The natural procedure by which the body and mind repairs*

8. **Horizon:** *Where problem meets solution*

9. **Harmony:** *The blend of peace, friendliness, and a cooperation of processes and life norms*

10. **Health:** *Habits that nourish and encourage physical, emotional, and mental wellness*

11. **Heritage:** *Practices and traditions passed down from one generation to the next*

12. **Honey:** *The small things in life that make life extra sweet*

13. **Humor:** *Even Jesus laughs, for laughing is good for the soul!*

14. **Heart:** *The inner emotion of love*

15. **Honor:** *Actions taken to honor God*

16. **Hands:** *The part of a person's body that displays his or her God-given crafts*

17. **History:** *Experience and what is learned from one's life*

18. **Harvest:** *A season in life when hard work pays off*

19. **Heaven:** *The earthly things that bring love and delight*

20. **Holy Spirit:** *The Spirit of God and Jesus Christ that guides us.*

Why Did God Create Women?

IN THE BEGINNING... God created a woman, primarily for Adam to have a companion. Women were created from the protective rib bone. But we all know when God does something, he goes all out. His creations are intentional and beautiful. For example, look around at the sky, the animals, the ocean, the human body. God meticulously and perfectly created all these things. Everything God creates is a majestic work of art, including you!

We all have things in our lives that detour our thinking and fogs God's true vision of what his purpose is for us. As women, living in today's world we continuously give, compromise, and put ourselves second to our careers and families. As caregivers, we sacrifice to give to others. As women, we negotiate, bite our tongues, and try to be everything to our loved ones. Oftentimes we run ourselves into the ground. During a period of my life, when I was a single mother, I was paying bills, and I thought, "I know God didn't create me just to pay bills. There has to be more to life than this?" I knew in my heart that God wanted more for me. I knew he created me for a purpose. God creates women with the same purpose and detail of the honeybee and the air we breathe. Women love and nurture the future. We often forget how special we really are. God created every woman with intentionality and in his image! We must never lose sight of that.

- 1 -
Hollowness

HOLLOWNESS: EMOTIONAL EMPTINESS
OR A CRAVING FOR SOMETHING MORE

WHEN I THINK about the word "hollowness," I see a deep, dark hole. So deep, when you throw something in there you never hear it hit the bottom. I choose to start with hollowness because most often this is where the trouble starts. We feel empty and yearn for something more. If we think about hollowness, what does it mean? It is emptiness and often a hole inside of us that we cannot fill. In Genesis 1:6 God said, "Let there be an expanse in the middle of the waters, and let it divide the waters from the waters." He called to the space to separate the water of earth from the water of the heavens. He called this space sky. How does the sky relate to the word "hollowness"? We cannot feel the sky, we cannot touch the sky, it's never-ending, and without God, that hollowness feels endless.

We often tell ourselves, "If I only made more money." "If I only had children." "If I could only find the right man." Why do we tell ourselves these things? "If I could only have a different life." Our thoughts spiral out of control, and we run around trying to fill this hole! We attempt to fill it with food, shopping, alcohol, sex, drugs, or any other distraction. When we are feeling hollow, we often distract ourselves to numb the pain or to avoid making the changes in our lives that God wants us to make. We fill the hole with distractions like overworking, overly scheduled calendars, excessive exercising, athletic events, or reading self-help books. There is nothing wrong with those things, I do them too, but God wants us to come to him when we are feeling hollow. When we put these things before God, they become a barrier. Marathon medals are not going to save you. CrossFit is not going to save you. Working long hours is not going save you. I have put each of these things before God at one point or another in my life. The world is full of harmless things that keep us from God. Even our desire to give our kids great lives, full of activities, can keep us from God. Why? Because we are too busy for God. We are trying to fill our own hollowness, which only God can fill. Nothing and no one should come between you and God. For some, this might sound a bit extreme, but it's true, and it is something I continue to work on myself. Remember, God wants us to come to him when we are feeling hollow.

Hollowness is related to the emptiness and loneliness we feel inside. Think about Jesus and his last hours filled with betrayal. Reflect upon his journey to the cross. He was betrayed by those closest to him. He walked alone carrying his cross while strangers mocked him. Imagine how he felt. He was still human. I am sure he felt broken. I am sure he felt alone at times or misunderstood, but he kept praying to God. Even upon the cross, nailed, and tortured, he sought God. "Forgive them" he yelled, "for they know not what they do" (Luke 23:34). When we feel hollow and alone, remember to turn back to God because his love and peace will fill your hollow brokenness. Jesus was able to endure all because of God.

I am not broken.
I am filled with God's love!

1. How do you connect with God to fill your hollowness?

_____

_____

_____

2. What makes you feel hollow?

_____

_____

_____

3. Would forgiveness fill your hollowness?

_____

_____

_____

4. Is there something or someone you should remove from your life to help you make changes in your life?

_____

_____

_____

GOD, PLEASE FILL ME WITH YOUR LOVE, AND FILL MY HOLLOWNESS.

_____

_____

_____

_____

_____

_____

_____

_____

_____

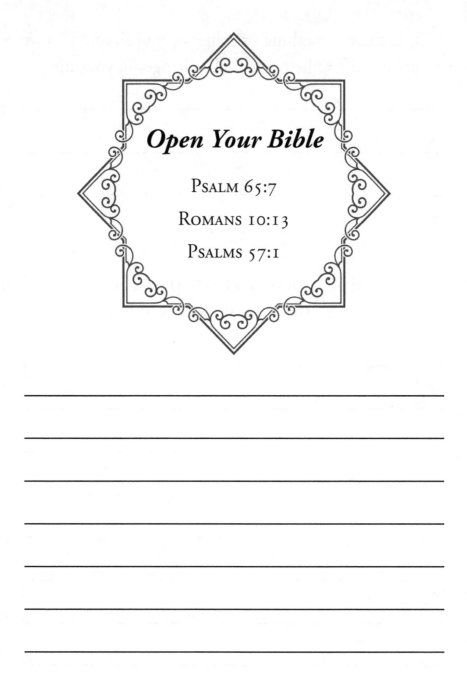

Open Your Bible

Psalm 65:7

Romans 10:13

Psalms 57:1

_____

_____

_____

_____

_____

_____

_____

_____

- 2 -
Harmful

HARMFUL: ANYTHING THAT HARMS YOU EMOTIONALLY OR PHYSICALLY

THERE ARE TWO types of harm: (1) external harm afflicted by others and (2) self-inflicted harm. We never wake up ready to be hurt or to damage our lives. Things happen quickly, like sand slipping through your fingers. For example, Jesus went from eating dinner to being crucified. What led to Jesus's crucifixion? Envy, fear, ignorance, lack of faith? People mocked him, and others feared that he would take over. There are things and people in our lives that are harmful to us and their negativity pierce us like the nails that pierced Jesus's hands. But death could not break him.

Every Christmas, the music director at my church does an awesome job with the Christmas program. The band, music, and skits are amazing, always reminding us about the true reason for Christmas, the baby Messiah. One year, there was video collection of testimonies where someone said, "I once was . . ., but through God, now

I'm…" Two dozen people participated that day. You can imagine the testimonies, the tears, and the cheers from the audience. And in the short moments of all those testimonies, the realization was painful. I felt like I was being hit by a car. My body was paralyzed. For the first time in my life, I realized all I was and had been. I wept uncontrollably. The people near me probably thought, "Wow, the Holy Spirit has really overcome her!" But it wasn't the Holy Spirit. It was shame. The shame of relating to every single testimony. I was thinking in my head, "God help me, I have been all those things!" "God, forgive me!" I cried and prayed and prayed and cried. What else could I do? God had removed the veil from my eyes, and I was now seeing the painful truth. I was seeing all the ways I was harming myself and had harmed others, while still dealing with my own personal wounds of betrayal. For the first time in my life, I saw all the harm I caused and experienced. My heart was in excruciating pain, and my head was pounding. I asked myself, "How am I going to make it to the car?" I felt like I had been struck by an eighteen-wheeler! We are quick to recognize the mistakes of others, but we are oblivious when it comes to our own.

The first recollection in the Bible of any "harm" was when Eve took a bite from the forbidden apple. This disobedience opened her eyes and Adam's eyes to sin. Once the apple was bitten, everything changed. All God wanted was for them not to eat from a specific tree. He did not want to deprive her; he wanted to protect her from harm, but the devil led Eve astray. The devil is only there to harm.

Another example of harm within the Bible was in Matthew 2:8, when King Herod called for a private meeting with the wise men. Herod said, "Go and search diligently for the young child. When you have found him, bring me word, so that I also may come and worship him." But he did not want to worship the baby Messiah. He wanted to harm him, just as there are people in our lives who don't care for us, don't want the best for us; they want to harm us because they're angry, they're hurt, they don't like us, and in their eyes, we don't deserve God's favor or God's blessings. They fail to realize judgments only come from God. When you harm others, repent, and ask for forgiveness. When someone has harmed you, pray for peace and give that person the same mercy God gives you. When you realize you have harmed yourself, pray for God to help you and guide you. When you are connected to God, Jesus, and the Holy Spirit, you will always be protected. On the next page, there are three columns: Broken Pottery, Resurrection, and Fruit of the Spirit. The first lists things that break us. The second, Resurrection, is a list of what can save us and restore us back to life. Lastly is Fruit of the Spirit, which is the gold that fills our brokenness.

On the next page, you may reflect on your own personal journey. Choose by circling, highlighting, or just picking one or two words to close your eyes and pray over. Feel free to make notes, draw pictures, or create anything that is symbolic to you.

_____

_____

_____

_____

_____

_____

_____

_____

_____

_____

_____

_____

_____

Broken Pottery	Resurrection	Fruit of the Spirit
Greed	Repent/Confess	Love
Excessive Vanity	Have Faith	Joy
Infertility	God's Love Heals	Peace
Drug and Alcohol Abuse	Ask for Mercy	Patience
Pornography	Give Control to God	Kindness
Resentment & Anger		Goodness
Lies		Faith
Abortion		Gentleness
Depression		Self-Control
Sexual Experimentation		
Giving Up a Child		
Excessive Debit		
Eating Disorders		
Mental, Physical, and Sexual Abuse		
Guilt		
Body Shame		
Incarceration		
Theft		
Regret		
Illness		
Adultery		
Eating Disorder		
Rape		
The Death of a Loved One		
Uncontrollable Spending		
Prostitution		
Addiction		

I'm not broken.
God's love protects me!

1. What are the harmful things in your life?

2. How can you remove them?

3. Is there someone in your life who is contributing to the harmful things in your life?

GOD, REMOVE THE HARMFUL THINGS FROM MY LIFE!

_____

_____

_____

_____

_____

_____

_____

_____

_____

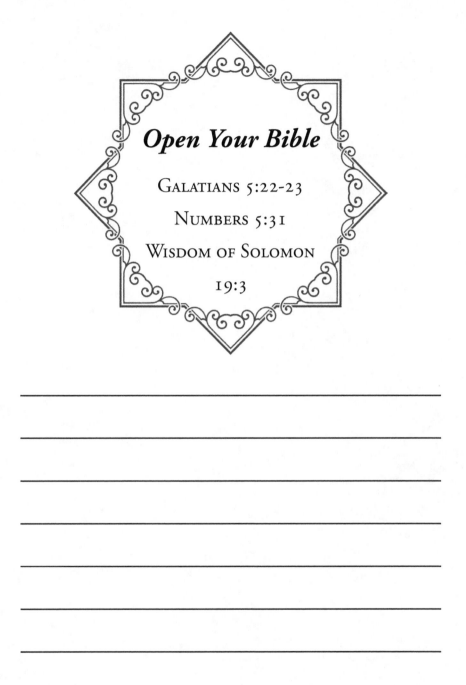

Open Your Bible

GALATIANS 5:22-23

NUMBERS 5:31

WISDOM OF SOLOMON

19:3

_____

_____

_____

_____

_____

_____

_____

_____

- 3 -

Hopelessness

HOPELESSNESS: GIVING UP OR THE
BELIEF THINGS CANNOT IMPROVE

HOPELESSNESS OFTEN SETS in when we feel like we are out of options, but if you think about it, extreme exhaustion often causes hopelessness. The exhaustion sets in when you are out of options, out of ideas, and out of resources. In the Bible, the first person who comes to my mind is Job. Job was a good man. He lived a blessed life, but without notice, Job was about to lose everything he ever had: his children, his wealth, and his health. Why did Job suffer such a tragedy? Because God challenged him just like he challenges us; he wanted to see how obedient and how strong Job's faith was.

It all started when God presented Job to Satan as an example of unshakable faith. "There is none like him in the earth, a perfect and an upright man, one that feared God and eschewed evil" (Job 1:8). No, God was not punishing Job for any sin; quite the opposite, he was using Job as an example, even as a trophy. Job suffered because he was among the best. He could not and would not forsake God. Satan, though, told Job that God didn't love him and tried to instigate him after Job lost his family, his daughters, his wife, his wealth. As he lay there on a heap of ashes, emotionally alone and confused, three friends came to comfort him, but instead emotionally and verbally prosecuting him. Job thought he was finished, doomed to die. He was broken down, lonely and felt hated. Job was hopeless. At one point, he moans, "My days are past, my purposes are broken off, even the thoughts of my heart, if I wait, the grave is mine." Even though Job had done nothing wrong and he desperately begged for help, God still chose to stay hidden. "I cry out to you, oh God, but you did not answer." But Job never gave up; he never stopped believing in God, and God blessed him twice as much as he had before, with twice as many sheep, twice as many camels and oxen; he even had seven sons and three daughters and lived a long life.

When we run out of options, or we run out of money, or we run out of energy, the one thing we can never run out of is God's love. There's no reason to feel hopeless when you have faith in God. With Christ, we are never out of options! When you feel like you are out of options, pray. Ask God to help you and guide you. When we try to handle things ourselves, things have a crazy way of getting out of control.

_____

_____

_____

_____

_____

_____

_____

_____

_____

_____

_____

_____

_____

I'm not broken. I am hopeful!

JESUS KNEW FOR some time that he was going to be crucified. In John 10:18 Jesus states, "No man taketh it from me, but I lay it down of myself. I have power to lay it down, and I have power to take it again." Jesus knew the long, hard journey ahead of him. In the world we live in now, knowing you are going to be ridiculed and killed could leave you hopeless. Job could have doubted God, but he believed in God's promise for him and his life. In the same way, there are struggles and emotions that hit like nails to the cross. They hurt. But don't feel hopeless. Like Jesus, believe in God's promise. "This commandment I received from my Father."

When we see ourselves the way God does, it changes our perspectives on all aspects of our lives. On the next page, really take a step back from everything going on in your life and complete the activity. Sometimes I like to close my eyes and take a few deep breaths. This helps me let go and let God.

Who am I through God?

WRITE A FEW WORDS DESCRIBING
WHO YOU ARE THROUGH GOD.

✝ I am…

_____

_____

_____

_____

_____

✝ Why?

_____

_____

_____

_____

_____

† When?

_____

_____

_____

_____

_____

† Where?

_____

_____

_____

_____

_____

✝ How?

_____

_____

_____

_____

_____

_____

✝ How can I increase this perspective in my life?

_____

_____

_____

_____

_____

_____

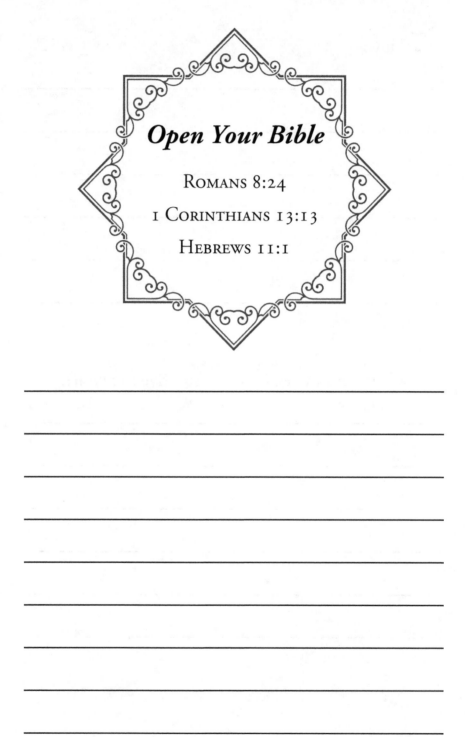

Open Your Bible

ROMANS 8:24

1 CORINTHIANS 13:13

HEBREWS 11:1

- 4 -
Hostage

HOSTAGE: THAT WHICH HOLDS BACK AND SHACKLES

HOSTAGE: THAT WHICH holds back and shackles because we live in a broken world, we all have things in our lives that hold us back from being what God has created us to be. What are some of those things in your life that shackle you and keep you hostage? There are many things in life that hold us hostage. It could be anger; it could be resentment; it could be that you are holding a grudge because you feel like you were treated unfairly; it could be an addiction that has a hold of you and won't let go; it could be a relationship that's holding you hostage that you just can't seem to get out of; it could be food—I know I've had those things show up in my life; it could also be ourselves—sometimes we are our own worst enemy. There's only one way to break those shackles, only one way to open up that gate of freedom, and that is with God, his Son, Jesus Christ, and the Holy Spirit. There's no other way. You cannot break free on your own, although we will try. I know from my personal experience that trying to do things on my own never gets me far. On the next page titled, 4 Ways to Break the Chains, there are four areas to reflect on, God's Support, Family Support, Self-Support, and a Community Support. Make a short list under each on how they can help you strengthen your faith and help set you free.

I'm not broken.
God's love sets me free!

1. What are some things that need to change in your life to break the shackles and bondage that hold you back from moving forward?

_____

_____

_____

2. What are the things in your life that can help you break free of the negative things that are bringing you down?

_____

_____

_____

3. What can you do to stay free from bondage?

_____

_____

_____

4 Ways to Break the Chains

WHAT ARE SOME WAYS THESE
FOUR SUPPORTS HELP YOU BREAK
THE CHAIN IN YOUR LIFE?

† God's Support

_____

_____

† Self-Support

_____

_____

† Family Support

_____

_____

† Community Support

_____

_____

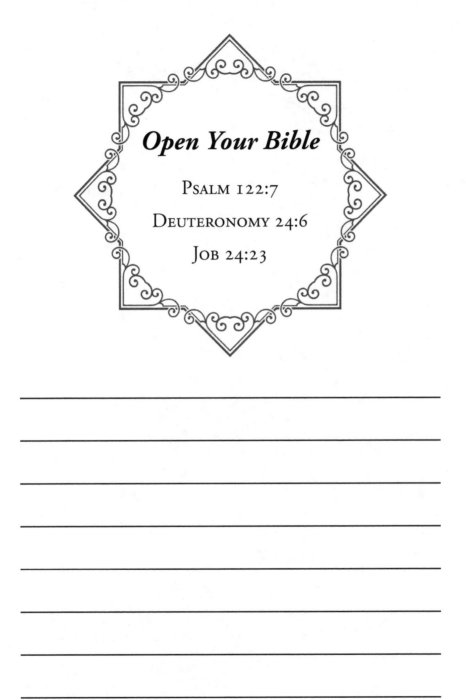

Open Your Bible

PSALM 122:7

DEUTERONOMY 24:6

JOB 24:23

_____

_____

_____

_____

_____

_____

_____

_____

_____

- 5 -
Humble

HUMBLE: MODESTY AND HAVING
A HUMBLE SELF-OPINION

BEING HUMBLE IS so important. Being humble is finding gratification in serving others. It doesn't matter how much money you have or how much money you don't have; it doesn't matter what school you went to; it doesn't matter how much education you have—everybody deserves to be treated fairly and respectfully. There is a saying that you must treat everybody from the janitor to the CEO with respect, and I hold that close to me. I will always believe and think that when you are humbled, you're willing to serve other people. And you are willing to say, "I don't know" or "I'm not sure if I can." You must be honest and transparent.

I think the biggest thing about being humble is Jesus Christ. When you think about Jesus Christ, and how God brought him to us here on earth to be the sacrificial lamb, he didn't bring Jesus here with the crown on his head. Jesus wasn't born into a prestigious family. He was born with livestock in the same small dusty room. I think God wanted us to see that his Son is just like you and me. I think God was sending an intentional message to us. I think he wanted to say, "Hey, I love you. You are part of me. Look at my son, He is just like you!" Growing up, Jesus was not wealthy. He didn't walk around thinking He was above everybody, even though He was and forever will be. God was so intentional of the picture He was painting for us. God painted a picture of love and humility. Jesus grew to be a strong passionate teacher. Today, we love and respect teachers. They are the foundation of humbleness because they love, nurture, and service learners.

I believe our children learn from their teachers the most besides their parents. Being humble is being willing to serve others, and I think that is an awesome and price-less trait. I prefer to serve the people around me. For example, whenever we have a dinner or a luncheon at work, I always stand up, and I make sure I serve every-body. I look around and make sure everybody has what they need, and I always eat last as a leader. I feel that it's important to make sure everybody else is situated and happy before I sit down. My mentality is always to serve, not to be served. I think the more I read about Jesus and deepen my understanding the more my heart and men-tality changed.

Why did God do this? I think God was trying to

connect with us. He was trying to humble himself by saying, "I am going to give the world my only son and he is just like you, made in my image." I think God was trying to show us that there was nothing wrong with being humble. Jesus was born in a modest manger, and he would soon share with the world God's vision for us, his knowledge, and his humbleness.

_____

_____

_____

_____

_____

_____

_____

_____

_____

_____

I'm not broken.
I am humble.

COMPLETE THE SENTENCES

✝ I serve others by…

_____

✝ Being humble is important because…

_____

✝ I am humble because…

_____

✝ Everyone is equal because…

_____

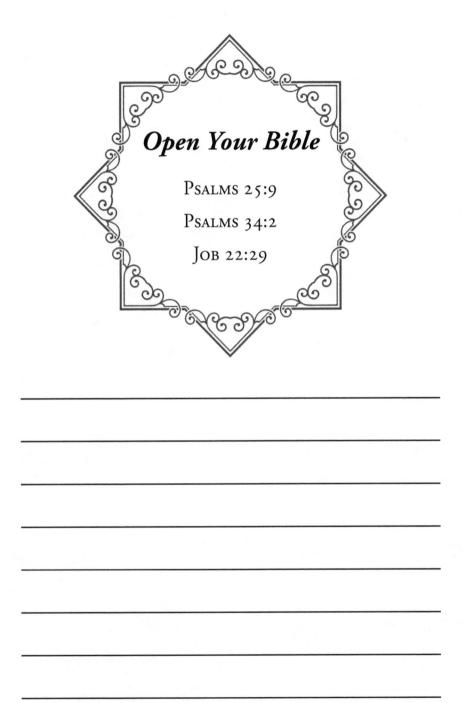

Open Your Bible

PSALMS 25:9

PSALMS 34:2

JOB 22:29

- 6 -
Honesty

HONESTY: HONOR AND RESPECT FOR THE TRUTH

WHY HONESTY? THERE are two reasons we need to be honest. We need to be honest with God and ourselves, so we can repent and find peace. Honesty to God, yourself, and others should remove the layer of lies and open your eyes to things you don't want to see and help you to follow through with decisions when they are hard or painful. When I think about honesty in the Bible, I think about how Joseph, in Genesis 37, was sold into slavery by his brothers. The truth was Joseph had a hard life. He was wrongfully sold into slavery. Potiphar's first wife accused him of rape after he denied her request to sleep with him. He was in jail because of his honesty. Sometimes honesty is a hard thing. It's difficult, it's hard to say, it's hard to hear. It's hard sometimes to understand what I am really mad about, what I am really depressed about. Is it me, or is it somebody else?

It's easy to blame somebody else when things go wrong; it's easy to blame somebody else when we're hurt, but we really need to be honest with ourselves, and we should be honest with God in order to move forward with our lives and accept everything that is waiting for us, such as his blessings and guidance. It is so important that we see things for what they are. It is easy to say we need to see everything through God's eyes, but the reality is that God can see everything and we cannot. We need to be honest with ourselves and with God. The only way to truly do this is by repenting. Some people feel comfortable telling a trusted church figure, and some do not. But what is most important is that you are honest with God and yourself. No excuses. No candy-coating it. Pure and simple. "I did, or I didn't, when I should have." "God, my actions were ugly, and I had a mean heart. God, I am angry and was ugly to my family. God, I have been lusting over another man. God, I am angry because I honestly believe that I deserve better. God, I did not give my best today." Whatever it is, it isn't so bad that God will not forgive you. The biggest thing I hear about honesty is "I am honest." Yes, but we are all sinners, and we can start by admitting that.

I'm not broken.
I am honest with God.

ADD YOUR HONEST STATEMENT.

✝ I am not perfect. I will never be. I am just a sinner who loves and believes in God.

_____

_____

_____

_____

✝ I must set aside personal space to pray, to mediate, and to spend time with God.

_____

_____

_____

_____

✝ I will not rely on my own understanding, but instead I will seek God for counsel.

_____

_____

_____

_____

_____

_____

_____

_____

_____

_____

_____

✝ I know there are things I need to change in my life, and I know God will help me.

I will not rely on my own understanding, but instead, I will seek God for counsel.

I will always try to be better than I was yesterday because I am Gods art in progress.

_____

_____

_____

_____

✝ I will always try to be better than I was yesterday because I am Gods art in progress.

_____

_____

_____

_____

Open Your Bible

PROVERBS 24:26

JOB 6:25

DEUTERONOMY 25:15

_____

_____

_____

_____

_____

_____

_____

_____

- 7 -
Healing

HEALING: THE NATURAL PROCEDURE BY WHICH THE BODY AND MIND REPAIRS

OFTENTIMES WE TRY to heal ourselves through shopping, sex, alcohol, eating, or spending money we don't have, trying to make ourselves feel better. We have all tried to self-heal or self-medicate in one way or another. I knew a young mom who was unhappy. She was in a loveless marriage with three young kids. She would buy extremely expensive clothes and the best shoes for her small children. They attended every class she could sign them up for, such as toddler tumbling, cooking, and swimming. These babies had no idea what their clothes cost and why they spent more time in car seats being shuttled around than at home together. While there is nothing wrong with wanting nice things for your children or providing them with enrichment, the truth was deep inside she was depressed and couldn't stand to be home. She was running away from her unhappiness, she confessed. You can never run away from your problems and expect to heal or fix things.

In the last chapter, we talked about honesty. I know for some that's the hardest chapter. I know it was for me because I was blind to some things I needed to be honest about. At times, it seemed okay because no one else knew how I was feeling or what I was going through. There wasn't enough food I could eat or enough shoes I could buy that could make me happy. I could not heal myself. Only God, His Son, and the Holy Spirit can heal us. Nothing else. And it's a process. At the back of the book there is a section with prayer pages. There, you can write your daily prayers to God. It is a good way to reflect and be intentional with your heart and your thoughts. Take some time to complete the activity through reflection and meditation and fill in the blanks! Remember, this is your book. There is no right or wrong answer.

Prayer

Dear sweet, loving King of Peace, help me heal. Help me to be strong in faith. Remove the veil from my eyes, so I can see things the way you do. I yearn to be better. I yearn to move forward on the path that you have laid for me. Please guide me on to the next chapter of my life.

_____

_____

_____

_____

_____

_____

_____

_____

_____

_____

Healing Activities

Spend time in your positive and fulfilling relationships. Cry in the shower, join a Bible study group, volunteer, get a massage, swim, run, bike, hike, walk, fast from food or spending, lead grace or prayer, coach a children's team, listen to the Bible on your way to work, and surround yourself with family and friends.

I'm not broken.
I am healing.

_____

_____

_____

_____

_____

_____

_____

Me	My problems, sin, addiction	How can I defeat the darkness?	Healing: How can I move forward?
EXAMPLE: ME	Financial Debt	Financial Fast Budget	Stay on a Planned Budget
Me at home			
Me at work			
Me and my family members			
Me and my faith			

I'm not broken.
I am healed through my faith!

1. God forgives our sins.

2. He gives us abundantly more than we ask for.

3. He shows us mercy, so we can show mercy to others.

4. He redeems us and makes us new again through His Son, Jesus Christ.

5. He guides us toward greener pastures.

6. God will turn the things that have come against us for our good.

7.

8.

9.

10.

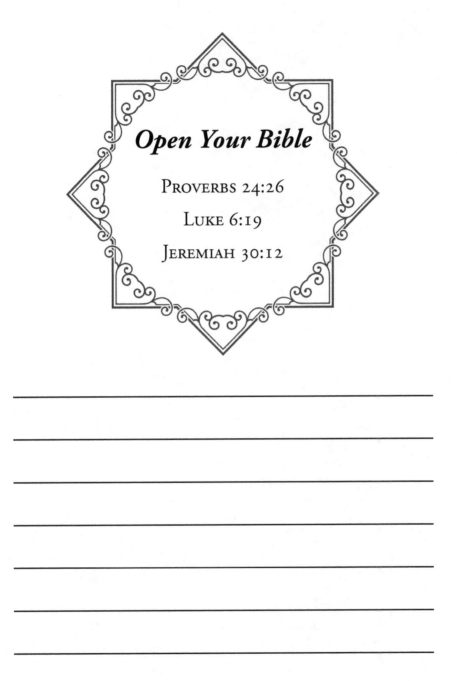

Open Your Bible

PROVERBS 24:26

LUKE 6:19

JEREMIAH 30:12

_____

_____

_____

_____

_____

_____

_____

_____

_____

- 8 -
Horizon

Horizon: Where problem
meets solution

WHEN THE DARK touches light. When the sun says, "Good night," and tucks itself into the ocean for bed. When the sky kisses the earth. That is the horizon. Why did God create the horizon? When I think about the horizon, I think about being lost at sea and finally seeing land! The horizon is when the storm is ending, and the pieces are finally falling into place. Those times in our lives when we see no way out and God opens a door. When we find ourselves in trouble and God closes the mouth of the lion. When you just don't know how you're going to make it and suddenly the pieces of the puzzle just fall into place. If you look up the word "horizon" in the Merriam-Webster Dictionary, there are two definitions. The first states that "the horizon is the line at which the earth's surface and the sky appear to meet." The second definition is "the limit of a person's mental perception, experience, or interest." They both describe a midpoint. Or in one's life, you could call it a transition.

When you arrive at the "horizon" period of your life, you are in a place where the storm has settled. You have been honest with God and yourself. You have a different perspective on life and how you want to live. You know the changes that need to be made. And most importantly, you have made a decision to let God guide your life. During the horizon phase of life, you are ready and eager to keep moving toward the cross. You acknowledge that life is not perfect, but you understand faith will get you through it. That is the horizon. It's a faithful outlook on life and a wholehearted desire to seek God and His Word and implement it in your life.

Pray, Reflect & Write

✝ I visualize…_____

✝ I hear…_____

✝ I feel…_____

✝ I think…_____

I'm not broken. God is my sun and shining light!

_____…makes the sun rise!

_____…helps me feel better!

_____…helps me look better!

_____…touches my heart!

_____…helps me move forward!

_____…heals my soul!

_____
_____…helps me treat the people around me better!

_____
_____…helps me see things through God's perspective!

_____…makes me better!

_____
_____…helps me see the best in others!

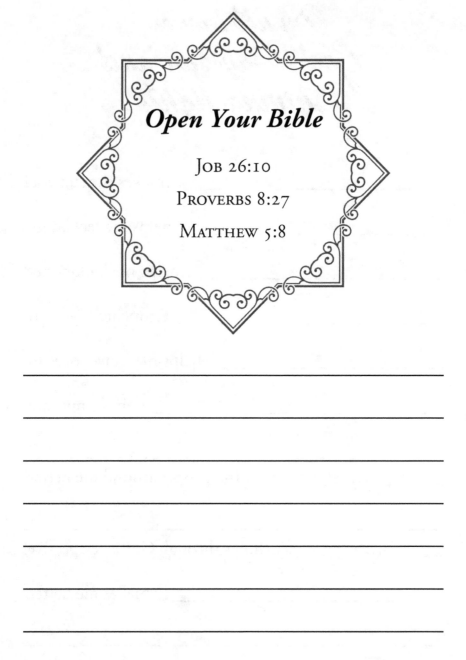

Open Your Bible

JOB 26:10

PROVERBS 8:27

MATTHEW 5:8

_____

_____

_____

_____

_____

_____

_____

_____

- 9 -
Harmony

HARMONY: THE BLEND OF PEACE, FRIENDLINESS, AND A COOPERATION OF PROCESSES AND LIFE NORMS

HARMONY IS MUSIC, laughter, the sound of the rain, the smooth flow of our everyday routines, the smooth flow of energy, and life moving forward like a well-oiled locomotive. Harmony is a song or a tune that makes your heart sing. It brings peace and contentment. Harmony is when everything seems to be going in the right direction. Harmony can be heard in the birds and in the wind. Harmony is all around us. The ocean also hums its signature tune. Sometimes, in seasons of hardship, we are so consumed with the negativity that we cannot hear God singing. When we are experiencing hardships, it doesn't mean there's no harmony; if you stop, listen, and remain still, you can hear your elders humming, the babbling of a baby, the roaring of the ocean. All those things are harmony. All those things are God singing to you.

Pray, Reflect & Write

✝ What does it mean to be a child of God?

_____

_____

_____

✝ What does harmony look like in your life?

_____

_____

_____

✝ With the world constantly coming at you, how does one maintain harmony in everyday life?

_____

_____

_____

I'm not broken.
I hear God in the
birds and wind.

I WILL LIVE WITH A PEACEFUL HEART!

✝ Harmony is…

_____

_____

✝ Harmony feels like…

_____

_____

✝ Harmony looks like…

_____

_____

✝ Harmony is given…

_____

_____

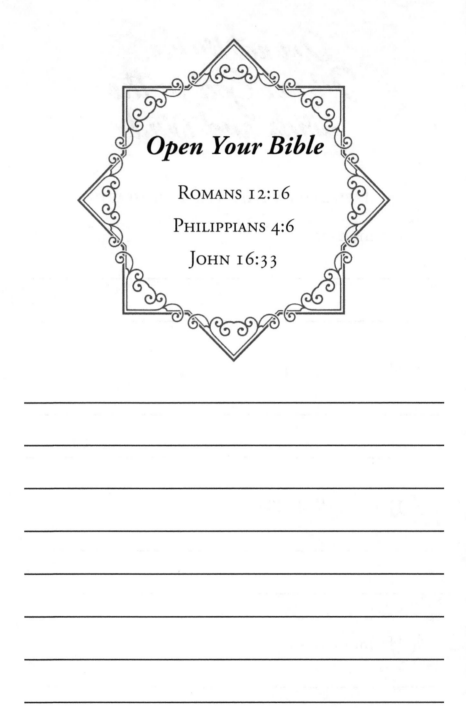

Open Your Bible

ROMANS 12:16

PHILIPPIANS 4:6

JOHN 16:33

_____

_____

_____

_____

_____

_____

_____

_____

- 10 -

Health

HEALTH: HABITS THAT NOURISH AND ENCOURAGE PHYSICAL, EMOTIONAL, AND MENTALLY WELLNESS

GOD CREATED EVERYTHING. On the first day, he created the sun, the moon, and the stars. On the second day, he created the birds and the fish. Then on the third day, he created animals and humans. When God created us, we were created in his image. We were created complete, whole, and full of peace, with nothing missing or broken. If you stop and think about how our bodies work, it is amazing how it heals itself and reproduces. We are God's masterpiece! During the health phase, we are focused and intentionally seeking God in different aspects of our lives.

_____

_____

_____

My Health	How can I incorporate these things into my life?	What Does The Bible Say?
Meditation: Walking with God ✝		
Diet: If God Didn't Make It, Don't Eat It 🍽		
Bible: Fill my mind with God's word 📖		
Heart: Exercise a grateful... ♥		

I'm not broken. After my body is gone, my soul will live on forever!

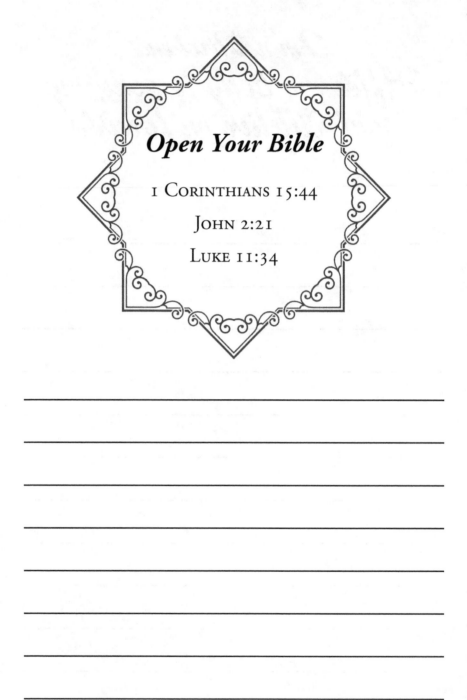

Open Your Bible

1 Corinthians 15:44

John 2:21

Luke 11:34

_____

_____

_____

_____

_____

_____

_____

_____

- 11 -
Heritage

HERITAGE: PRACTICES AND TRADITIONS PASSED DOWN FROM ONE GENERATION TO THE NEXT

SOMETIMES GOD CALLS us to do things. I don't think it's always majestic. It can be a nudge or tug. Those things can be to get married, change careers, serve our country in the military, stay home with our children, extend our family, or maybe take care of an elder family member. When he calls us to do something, there is always something he wants us to learn and leave behind. For example, a message, a lesson, an understanding. We also leave behind the memories of a long marriage rooted in faith for young love to follow. We leave behind a legacy of courage and honor. You may also leave behind respect, love, and selflessness at a job or business. Our heritage are the practices and traditions passed down from one generation to the next through life lessons and faith. Isaiah 54:17, "No weapon that is formed against thee shall prosper; and every tongue that shall rise against thee in judgment thou shalt condemn. This is the heritage of the servants of the Lord, and their righteousness is of me, said the Lord."

This is one of my favorite verses because it reminds me of the heritage that God has left behind for me through his Son, Jesus Christ. It makes me feel loved and protected. And it reminds me that I belong to the family of the one true King of all. Look and reflect on the family tree on the next pages. Nothing is a coincidence.

PRAY, REFLECT & WRITE

† What are some strengths you have inherited from your family's heritage?

† Who in your past has changed your path in life?

† What is the heritage you are starting?

† What is in your heart that you want to leave behind?

† Are you building your lineage of chain or rope? Why?

† What are some weak links in your heritage that you can make better?

What I Inherited and from Whom	What I Hope to Pass on and to Whom

The 12 Nations of Israel Family Tree

ABRAHAM MARRIED SARAH

ISAAC, THE SON, MARRIED REBEKAH

JACOB, THE SON, MARRIED RACHEL,
LEAH, BILIAH, ZILPAH

The 12 Nations of Israel

(THE CHILDREN OF JACOB)
REUBEN, SIMEON, LEVI, JUDAH,
ISSACHAR, ZEBULUN, DAN, NAPHTALI,
GAD, ASHER, JOSEPH, AND BENJAMIN

I'm not broken.
I will leave a legacy of faith and goodness.

_____

_____

_____

_____

_____

_____

_____

_____

_____

_____

_____

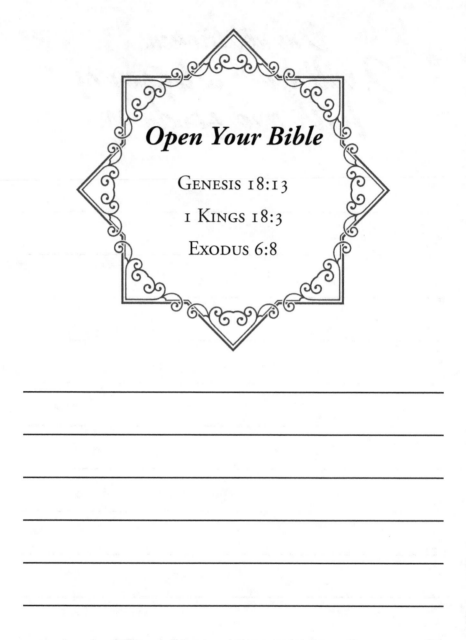

Open Your Bible

GENESIS 18:13

1 KINGS 18:3

EXODUS 6:8

_____

_____

_____

_____

_____

_____

_____

_____

- 12 -
Honey

HONEY: THE SMALL THINGS IN LIFE
THAT MAKE LIFE EXTRA SWEET

HONEY AND THE Promised Land were promised to the people of Israel. The land of milk and honey made me think about and want to hold on to all the sweet things in my life. There is honey in our everyday lives, but we must choose to see it. Honey can be when you pull up to pay for your coffee and the server tells you the car in front of you already paid for it. That is honey! When God saves you from the fire, that is honey! Your AC goes out and you think, "How am I going to pay for a new air conditioner?" and the repairman tells you, "Oh, it's only going to be a fifty-dollar part." That is honey! These are not coincidences in your life; these are God's sweet blessings.

I'm not broken.
God blesses me every day!

COUNT YOUR BLESSINGS.

1 _____

_____

_____

2. _____

_____

_____

3. _____

_____

_____

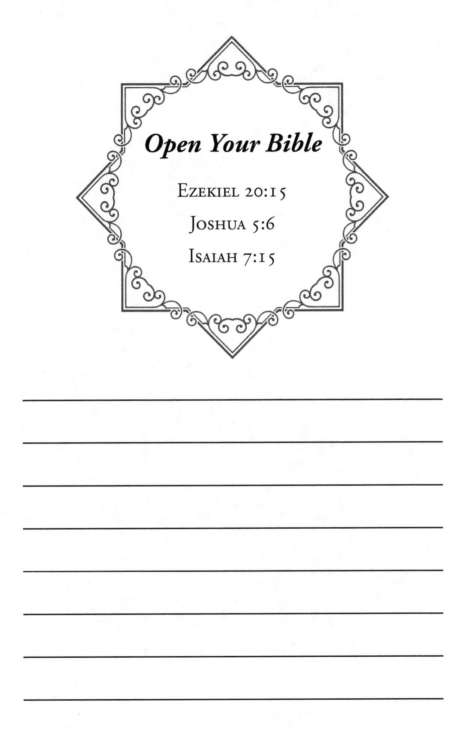

Open Your Bible

EZEKIEL 20:15

JOSHUA 5:6

ISAIAH 7:15

_____

_____

_____

_____

_____

_____

_____

_____

_____

- 13 -
Humor

HUMOR: EVEN JESUS LAUGHS, FOR LAUGHING IS GOOD FOR THE SOUL!

I THINK OFTEN there is a misconception about God. I think in our heads we see him up in the clouds, ready to strike us with lightning and punish us if we blink wrong. That cannot be further from the truth. When I think of God, I think of him as a father figure. As family, we go through the highs and lows together. We celebrate together, we cry together, we laugh, and poke fun at each other. I think God is the same way. The Bible talks about all the things that bring him joy. Sometimes I hear God laughing with me and sometimes comforting me the same way my family does. Science says that laughing secretes chemicals in the brain that make us feel good. We also know that laughing is good for our health and our souls. God is our loving father who wants to laugh and be joyful with us.

I'm not broken. I have a happy heart that loves the Lord!

Think about a time when you laughed hard. In order to relive the moment, take a few minutes to call someone who was there; tell them how grateful you are for that memory.

Memory of Laughter	My Emotion and Feeling
Memory of Laughter	My Emotion and Feeling
Memory of Laughter	My Emotion and Feeling

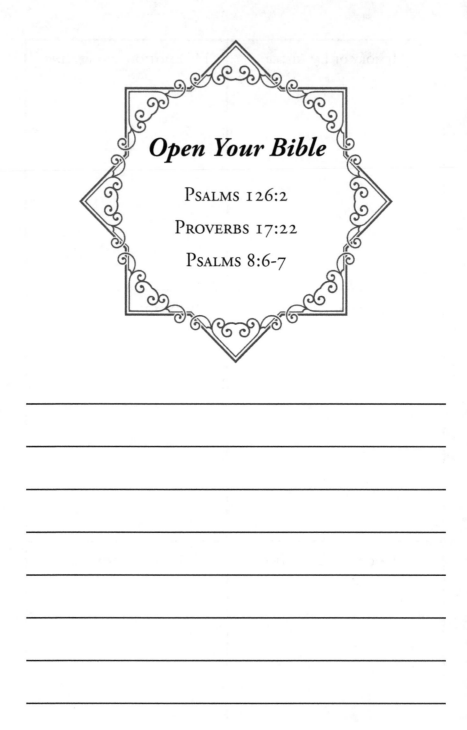

Open Your Bible

PSALMS 126:2

PROVERBS 17:22

PSALMS 8:6-7

_____

_____

_____

_____

_____

_____

_____

_____

- 14 -
Heart

HEART: THE INNER EMOTION OF LOVE

THERE IS NO doubt that what is inside of us comes from the one true God. It is not a coincidence that our hearts are in the center of our bodies. Even though our hearts are muscles, they still represent love, emotions, and goodness. The heart is a strong muscle scientifically, but emotionally it is the most fragile. It can be broken, hurt, cold, and scientifically can stop at any time without notice. The heart is a very complex organ. Back in the ancient times, it was thought that we used our hearts to think. Let God into your heart, and watch your life change.

_____

_____

_____

_____

I'm not broken.
God fills my heart with...

❤ JESUS, HEAL MY HEART!	❤ JESUS, OPEN MY HEART!	❤ JESUS, FILL ME HEART!
WHAT ARE SOME THINGS YOU CAN DO TO HEAL?	WHAT ARE SOME THINGS YOU CAN DO TO OPEN YOUR HEART?	WHAT ARE SOME THINGS YOU CAN FILL YOUR HEART WITH?
♪	♪	♪
📖	📖	📖

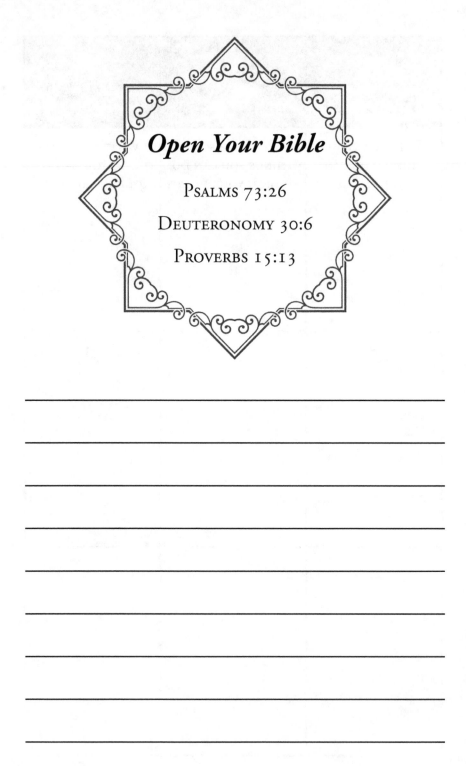

Open Your Bible

PSALMS 73:26

DEUTERONOMY 30:6

PROVERBS 15:13

_____

_____

_____

_____

_____

_____

_____

_____

_____

- 15 -
Honor

HONOR: ACTIONS TAKEN TO HONOR GOD

AT MY CHILDREN'S school, they have a computer program where I can log on and check their grades at any time. One day my son says, "Mom, I don't know why you keep checking my grades, it always upsets you." And I said, "Well, you're my son, you're my responsibility, and I'm going to keep checking to make sure that you are doing what you need to be doing!" I was upset with him because a few grades were low. He responded back by saying, "You know, it's so hard to do good in that class because the teacher's so boring." And I interjected, "You need to listen to that teacher like its God coming down from the sky and speaking to you! You wouldn't be bored if God was teaching the class." Everything you do should be done unto the Lord. If you think about honor, we can honor a lot of things. We can honor our families, our jobs, and our communities. God wants us to honor everything he puts in our paths and make significant contributions to the world.

Pray, Reflect & Write

✝ How are you honoring the gifts God has given you?

✝ How are you honoring the life that was given to you?

✝ How are you honoring the relationships God has given you?

_____

_____

_____

_____

_____

_____

_____

_____

_____

Pray, Reflect & Write

What are the four things in your life that you need to honor intentionally?

1.

_____

_____

_____

2.

_____

_____

_____

3.

_____

_____

_____

4.

_____

_____

_____

I'm not broken.
I live a life that honors God!

My Actions	How do my actions honor God?
My Time	
My Health	
My Heart	
My Mind	
My Family	
My Money	
My Goals	
My Hands	

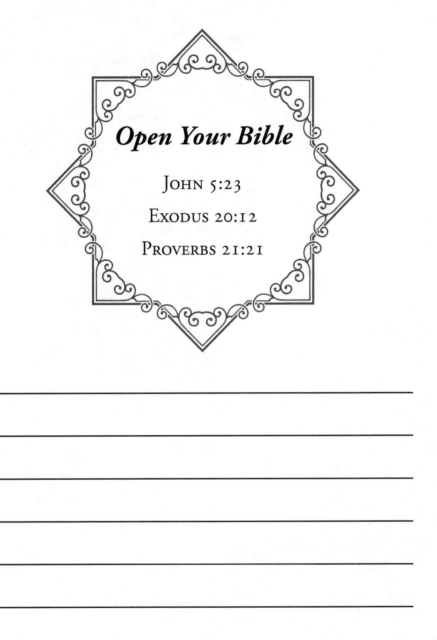

Open Your Bible

John 5:23

Exodus 20:12

Proverbs 21:21

_____

_____

_____

_____

_____

_____

_____

_____

- 16 -
Hands

HANDS: THE PART OF A PERSON'S BODY THAT DISPLAYS HIS OR HER GOD-GIVEN CRAFTS

I THINK THIS chapter is especially wonderful because "hand" is a bit of a curveball for some. I know hands are kind of an odd thing to talk about, but it came to my mind because I thought about Jesus being pierced on the cross with these huge nails in his hands. I was trying to imagine all the things that he might have felt, and then I thought to myself, "Could I have gone through the same crucifixion with the same grace and mercy?" Then my next thought was, I wonder what Jesus's hands look like because he was a carpenter. My dad was also a carpenter, and I remember his hands were hard and scarred. I know that's kind of odd, but I think "hands" are under-recognized. And they are significant. Jesus blessed others with his hands, he performed miracles with his hands, and he washed people's feet with his hands. Hands are so significant!

What are you doing with your hands to honor God? Are you serving others? Are you hugging and blessing the people you love? Why did God give us hands? We use our hands to pray, to work, to hold, to cook, to clean, to make, to comfort, to write, to carry. Let your hands be blessings to others.

Open your Bible.	What do I think?	What do I feel?
Acts 19:11 "God worked special miracles by the hands of Paul, 12 so that even handkerchiefs or aprons were carried away from his body to the sick, and the evil spirits went out."		
Isaiah 64:8 "But now, God, you are our Father. We are the clay, and you our potter. We all are the work of your hand."		
Mark 5:28 "For she said, "If I just touch his clothes, I will be made well."		

I'm not broken.
God holds me in his hand.

WHAT ARE THE THINGS IN YOUR LIFE THAT YOU NEED TO PUT IN GOD'S HANDS?

1. Trace your hand.
2. Draw or note the things you
need to put in God's hands.

Open Your Bible

Exodus 15:6

Deuteronomy 28:8

Joshua 11:6

_____

_____

_____

_____

_____

_____

_____

_____

- 17 -
History

HISTORY: EXPERIENCE AND WHAT IS LEARNED FROM ONE'S LIFE

HISTORY STEMS FROM the series of events that have happened in life. Your history is your life and the things you've gone through and have overcome. The history of Jesus's life involves being born in a manger and then crucified for us to forgive our sins. When you stop and think about all the things He went through, you might question, "Why would such an awesome God let his only son go through all that?" But God always has (1) a bigger plan, (2) our best interest in mind, and (3) the strength to get us through anything. When I look back at my life, I used to wish I could go back and change things, but now, as I move closer to the cross, I embrace my God-given history. It has made me into the person I am today. I now live backward. I think about where I want to be and where I want to work, and I work on getting there. I live my life with the end in mind. When I die, I think I will see God's face, and even though He already knows my answer, He's going to ask me, "Christina, what did you do with the gifts I gave you? How did you help the people I put in your path? What did you do with the children I gave you?" I reflect on how I am spreading His Word and emulating His love and light. As I move forward into my history, I don't know what lies before me, but I do know that I want to have a history that shows I put God first.

I'm not broken.
God is directing my steps!

SET A SMALL GOAL AND NOTE YOUR PATH.

```
┌────────────────────────────────────┐
│                                    │
│                                    │
└────────────────────────────────────┘
                  ⇩
┌────────────────────────────────────┐
│                                    │
│                                    │
└────────────────────────────────────┘
                  ⇩
┌────────────────────────────────────┐
│                                    │
│                                    │
└────────────────────────────────────┘
                  ⇩
┌────────────────────────────────────┐
│                                    │
│                                    │
└────────────────────────────────────┘
                  ⇩
┌────────────────────────────────────┐
│                                    │
│                                    │
└────────────────────────────────────┘
                  ⇩
┌────────────────────────────────────┐
│                                    │
│                                    │
└────────────────────────────────────┘
```

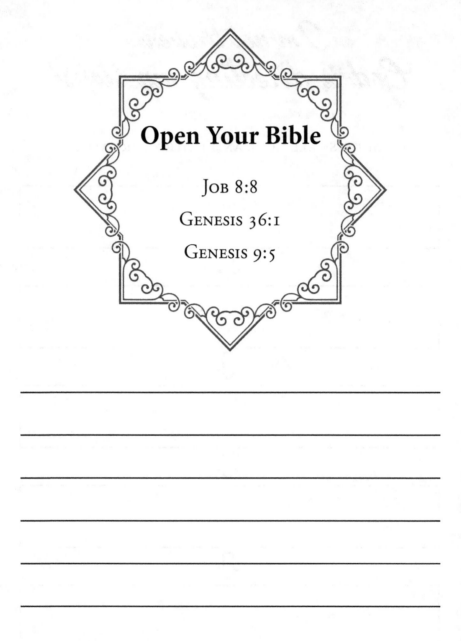

Open Your Bible

JOB 8:8

GENESIS 36:1

GENESIS 9:5

- 18 -
Harvest

HARVEST: A SEASON IN LIFE WHEN HARD WORK PAYS OFF

IN THE HARVEST phase, it is a time to harvest everything we have planted. It's time to reap the benefits from all our diligence and hard work, but the biggest misconception about the harvest phase is that all harvests are plentiful. If you talk to farmers, some harvests are huge, but some year's farmer lose everything. The mistake that we can often make is that we are not patient enough to wait for the harvest. There are times in our lives that we are passed up for jobs we are highly qualified for, or maybe betrayed by someone we love, but it's not our job to control everything or everyone. That is God's job. Let God fight your battles, and instead focus on doing what is right and on the harvest. As we are plowing the soil, pulling the weeds, and planting seeds, whether we have a good harvest or not, through faith we must keep going and to remain diligent where God has us.

In the book of Ruth, Boaz, a prominent man, and landowner tells his workers to leave extra wheat behind for Ruth to pick up later. There are two things I notice about Boaz: (1) He was calm and treated his workers with respect, and (2) he wasn't greedy with his harvest. In the end, God blessed him with a wife and son.

Open Your Bible

Mathew 13:1–9

_____

_____

_____

_____

_____

_____

_____

_____

THE FARMER SOWING SEED

MATTHEW 13:1 - 23

ON THAT DAY Jesus went out of the house and sat by the seaside. 2 Great multitudes gathered to him, so that he entered into a boat, and sat, and all the multitude stood on the beach. 3 He spoke to them many things in parables, saying, "Behold, a farmer went out to sow. 4 As he sowed, some seeds fell by the roadside, and the birds came and devoured them. 5 Others fell on rocky ground, where they didn't have much soil, and immediately they sprang up because they had no depth of earth. 6 When the sun had risen, they were scorched. Because they had no root, they withered away. 7 Others fell among thorns. The thorns grew up and choked them. 8 Others fell on good soil, and yielded fruit: some one hundred times as much, some sixty, and some thirty.

_____

_____

_____

_____

_____

I'm not broken.
God helps me grow!

What seed did God plant in me?	How did I nurture the seed?	What did I harvest?

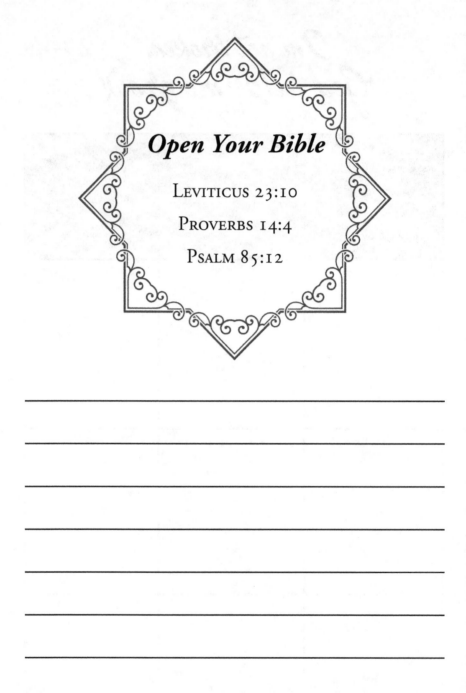

Open Your Bible

LEVITICUS 23:10

PROVERBS 14:4

PSALM 85:12

_____

_____

_____

_____

_____

_____

_____

_____

- 19 -
Heaven

HEAVEN: THE EARTHLY THINGS THAT BRING LOVE AND DELIGHT

LET ME TELL you a story about my grandmother. She was in love with a man named Tom. He was a tall classy Caucasian man. They spent time together walking around and talking. But when Tom approached his family about marrying her, he was forbidden. Can you imagine the courage it took for him to ask? I can imagine that deep inside he knew what his family reaction would be because my grandmother was Hispanic, but out of desperation, he asked for a family blessing. Tom probably had a better chance of getting struck by lightning. My grandmother was devastated. She later married a Navy Sailor, had four children but suffered at the hand of an alcoholic. There is even a family rumor that when my grandmother went into labor with my mom, she arrived at the hospital with a black eye. I only knew my grandmother at her best. She took care of and prayed for everyone who crossed her path.

She later was diagnosed with Alzheimer's disease. After a long fight, she was hospitalized and was given days to live. She called from the hospital one day, eager and smitten, and asked me to take her to buy a wedding dress. I humored her and went to see her that day after work. She asked me again. Like a little girl, she described her dress and knew the exact place she wanted it from. My mom was visiting my grandmother at the hospital. She just looked at me and gestured to me with her body to go along with it. I replied, "Yes, Grandma, of course, I will take you." She tried to get up, exclaiming that she did not want to be late. She was in a rush all of a sudden. I stopped her before she could get out of her hospital bed. I scolded her, "Where do you think you are going?" She said innocently, "I have to get my dress. Tom is coming for me." You see, Tom was her heaven. It was a love that never died. It was a love that she held onto. In my heart, I see her young and beautiful again running away with him in a lace wedding dress. I can see her laughing and smiling. After all the abuse, my grandmother had gone through, she deserved to be happy.

We all have a heaven. Something that brings us peace and keeps us going. For some people dying and going to heaven is a scary thing. There are many people who fear dying for many reasons. Some people fear the unknown, some people fear dying and leaving loved ones behind, and some fear death when they just aren't ready.

Although we live here on earth with wars and famine, heaven is all around us. We see it in the sky and the ocean. We see it in the birth of a baby. Heaven is all around us if we choose to see it. It is the same way with the pottery. You can see it as broken, or you can see it as a piece of art.

_____

_____

_____

_____

_____

_____

_____

_____

_____

_____

_____

I'm not broken.
One day I will touch Gods face!

My heaven is . . .

My heaven is . . .

My heaven is . . .

My heaven is . . .

My heaven is . . .

My heaven is . . .

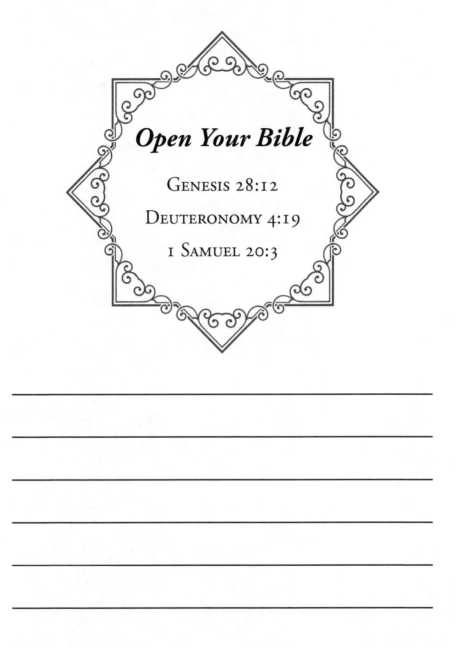

Open Your Bible

GENESIS 28:12

DEUTERONOMY 4:19

1 SAMUEL 20:3

_____

_____

_____

_____

_____

_____

_____

_____

_____

- 20 -
Holy Spirit

HOLY SPIRIT: THE SPIRIT OF GOD AND JESUS CHRIST THAT GUIDES US

WHEN I STARTED this journey to write a faith-based book, I was extremely torn. I was unsure of myself. I even argued with God. I asked, "God, why do you want me to write a book? I'm not perfect. I'm not the pope. I did not graduate from an awesome Bible school! I'm not a theologian. What do I know?" But, God knows everything. He knew me before I was born, conceived, or even a gleam in my father's eyes. He knew that I would write this book. The Holy Spirit put this on my heart. The journey of life is beautifully difficult. It's a roller coaster that I know so many of you have experienced. For me, the most difficult obstacle in life is always me. The difficulty of being human and surrendering control to God. I finally let go, and said, "Okay, God, if you want me to write this book, I will do it." One day I regressed back to doubt and asked God for a sign. I opened the Bible and there it was in Jeremiah. The Scripture said, "Take thee a scroll and write on it all the words I have spoken to thee" (Jeremiah 36:2). So, I proceeded in faith. This book was written to honor God and in hopes that I can encourage you to do what the Holy Spirit is nudging you to do. This is your sign if you have been asking for one.

HOLY SPIRIT, COME INTO MY...	HOLY SPIRIT, COME INTO MY...
HOLY SPIRIT, COME INTO MY...	HOLY SPIRIT, COME INTO MY...

I'm not broken.
The Holy Spirit is with me!

_____

_____

_____

_____

_____

_____

_____

_____

_____

_____

_____

_____

The Cracked Pot Folktale

THE STORY OF the cracked pot is a fable that has many interpretations from all over the world including the bible. This version is through the imagination of the author.

There was once an elderly woman that had two fat pots. Each pot hung lazily on the ends of a pole. Whenever she would retrieve water, she carried a pole across her shoulders with one fat pot on each end. One of the pots was flawless and proud, and always carried a full serving of water, and the other pot had a profound crack in it that would leak. At the end of the long walk from the brook to the house, the cracked pot ways made it home only half full.

For years, the woman used the fat pots for water. Making it home every day with one full pot and one with less than because of the crack. Of course, the flawless pot was proud of its accomplishments. But the cracked pot was ashamed of its imperfection and unhappy because it could only do half of what it had been created to do. Years passed by and one day the cracked pot spoke to the woman, "I am depressed and unhappy with myself because of my crack. It causes water to leak all the way back to your house. It makes me feel useless and shameful."

The old woman's face was warm and compassionate. She smiled and responded softly, "Did you see that there are beautiful flowers on only your side of the stone path, and not on the other side? Your crack bothers you, not me. One day, I had the idea to sprinkle flower seeds on your side of the path because I knew when we walked home from the brook you would water them and help them grow. For years, I have picked these beautiful flowers you watered from seeds. I use the flowers to decorate the table, give to my friends and neighbors, and honor the graves of the dead. Without your crack, I would not be able to bring joy and honor to others. Despite what you think of yourself, I appreciate you just the way you are." And the woman wrapped her delicate arms around the pot and hugged her. ♥

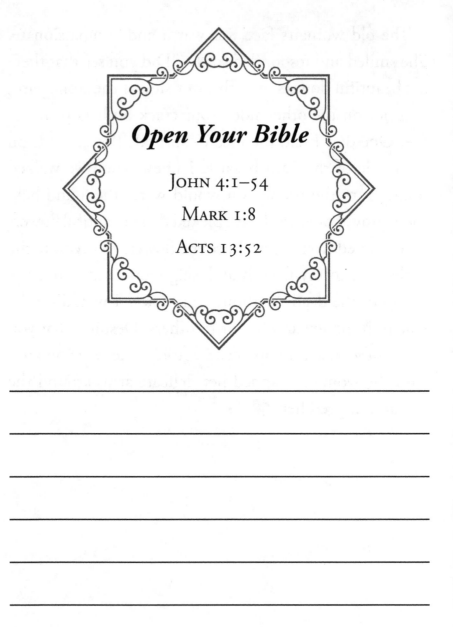

Open Your Bible

JOHN 4:1–54

MARK 1:8

ACTS 13:52

_____

_____

_____

_____

_____

_____

_____

_____

Conclusion

Of all the H's in the Bible, the one that brings me the most peace is "hope." I put my hope in God because the world has made it easy to accept broken relations, to accept negative thoughts, and to accept the darkness. Do not accept it. The world's perspective is meaningless in comparison to God's promise. We all have a tipping point. Where is the point where we stop hurting? When do we stop existing? Why do we drown ourselves in things of the world before going to God? Because we are human. I know I will never be perfect. I will forever be working on myself and my faith no matter how hard life gets. Faith is something that we can work on forever and we will never be worthy, but God loves us just the same. Be you, be all that God created you to be. Just as a broken pot, no matter how careful we are, eventually the pot will chip, crack, or break. But if we ask, God will always redeem us. There is always hope.

PSALMS 18:1
"I WILL LOVE THEE, LORD, MY STRENGTH."
MAY PEACE BE WITH YOU,

CHRISTINA DEMARA
LIFE · LEARNING · LEADERSHIP

Never Underestimate the Power of Prayer

_____

_____

_____

_____

_____

_____

_____

_____

_____

_____

_____

✟ Thank you, God, for the beautiful things you have created in the world. Today, I pray for peace.

_____

_____

_____

✟ Thank you, God, for loving and forgiving me. Today, I pray for guidance.

_____

_____

_____

✟ Thank you, God, for the good and bad in my life. I know you have a plan for me. Today, I pray that I may love myself the way you love me.

_____

_____

_____

✝ God, sometimes I stumble. I am sorry for my sins. Today, I pray for your forgiveness.

_____

_____

_____

✝ Thank you, God, for loving me. I pray to be more merciful. God, help me show others mercy the way you have shown me.

_____

_____

_____

✝ Thank you, God, for taking control of my life. I trust you.

_____

_____

_____

✝ God, help me move on from my past. Today, I pray for change in my life.

_____

_____

_____

✝ Thank you for blessing me. Today, I pray for the children in my life. That they may know and feel your love.

_____

_____

_____

✝ God, I pray for the men in my life. Please help them see the impact they make on others.

_____

_____

_____

✝ God, thank you for always doing what is best for me. Today, I pray for your protection from anyone who wishes me harm.

_____

_____

_____

✝ Thank you, God, for knitting me in my mother's womb. Today, I pray for forgiveness and your love.

_____

_____

_____

✝ Thank you, God, for always providing for me. I pray for you to break the shackles of debt in my life.

_____

_____

_____

✝ Thank you, God, for your grace. Today, I pray for wisdom.

_____

_____

_____

✝ Thank you, God, for today. I pray for a humble and giving heart.

_____

_____

_____

✝ God, help me be more like you. I pray for meaningful work and a sense of purpose.

_____

_____

_____

✝ God, I pray for a better tomorrow for all. Please guide my employer and community leaders.

_____

_____

_____

✝ Thank you, God, for putting me where I am in this moment with you. Today, I pray for wisdom and to see things the way you do.

_____

_____

_____

✝ God, only through you am I healed and at peace. Today, I pray for you to give me the strength to forgive others who have wronged me.

_____

_____

_____

✝ God, I want to be unselfish. Today, I pray for my needs and the needs of others.

_____

_____

_____

✝ God, I know that you are my shield and vindicator. Please help me move forward.

_____

_____

_____

✝ God, thank you for being a loving father and life mentor. Today, I pray for prosperity for myself and loved ones.

_____

_____

_____

✝ I pray to you, God, to help me see the good in all people the way you do.

_____

_____

_____

✝ Thank you, God, for everything you have blessed me with. Today, I pray for you to open the door to something new in my life.

_____

_____

_____

✝ God, through you, I can do anything! I pray for you to use me as a catalyst for change.

_____

_____

_____

✝ God, today, I pray for you to bless me with an open heart and an open mind so I may accept all that you have in store for my life.

_____

_____

_____

✝ God, help me heal. Today, I pray for the people who have hurt me.

_____

_____

_____

✝ I pray, God, for you to give me the strength to let go of all the things that are not helping me grow spiritually.

_____

_____

_____

✝ Thank you, God, for my relationships. I pray that you continue to put the right people in my path.

_____

_____

_____

NEVER UNDERESTIMATE
THE POWER OF PRAYER

_____

_____

_____

_____

_____

_____

_____

_____

_____

_____

_____

_____

20 H's	WHERE I AM CURRENTLY	WHERE I WANT TO BE
1. HOLLOWNESS: EMOTIONAL EMPTINESS OR A CRAVING FOR SOMETHING MORE		
2. HARMFUL: ANYTHING THAT HARMS YOU EMOTIONALLY OR PHYSICALLY		
3. HOPELESSNESS: GIVING UP OR THE BELIEF THINGS CANNOT IMPROVE		
4. HOSTAGE: THAT WHICH HOLDS BACK AND SHACKLES		
5. HUMBLE: MODESTY AND HAVING A HUMBLE SELF-OPINION		

20 H's	Where I Am Currently	Where I Want to Be
6. HONESTY: HONOR AND RESPECT FOR THE TRUTH		
7. HEALING: THE NATURAL PROCEDURE BY WHICH THE BODY AND MIND REPAIRS		
8. HORIZON: WHERE PROBLEM MEETS SOLUTION		
9. HARMONY: THE BLEND OF PEACE, FRIENDLINESS, AND A COOPERATION OF PROCESSES AND LIFE NORMS		
10. HEALTH: HABITS THAT NOURISH AND ENCOURAGE PHYSICAL, EMOTIONAL, AND MENTAL WELLNESS		

20 H's	Where I Am Currently	Where I Want to Be
11. Heritage: Practices and traditions passed down from one generation to the next		
12. Honey: The small things in life that make life extra sweet		
13. Humor: Even Jesus laughs, for laughing is good for the soul!		
14. Heart: The inner emotion of love		
15. Honor: Actions taken to honor God		

20 H's	Where I Am Currently	Where I Want to Be
16. HAND: The part of a person's body that displays his or her God-given crafts		
17. HISTORY: Experience and what is learned from one's life		
18. HARVEST: A season in life when hard work pays off		
19. HEAVEN: The earthly things that bring love and delight		
20. HOLY SPIRIT: The Spirit of God and Jesus Christ that guides us		

NEVER UNDERESTIMATE
THE POWER OF PRAYER

_____

_____

_____

_____

_____

_____

_____

_____

_____

_____

_____

_____

Reading Log

Facts about Characters:	This scripture made me realize…
Impactful Words:	I need to research…
Who could benefit from this Scripture?	I can visualize…
Symbolism:	Key Events:

WHAT DOES GOD WANT ME TO KNOW?	HOW DOES THIS SCRIPTURE CONNECT TO MY LIFE?
IMPACTFUL VERSE:	KEY TAKEAWAYS:
IMPACTFUL VERSE:	KEY TAKEAWAYS:
IMPACTFUL VERSE:	KEY TAKEAWAYS:

READING LOG

FACTS ABOUT CHARACTERS:	THIS SCRIPTURE MADE ME REALIZE...
IMPACTFUL WORDS:	I NEED TO RESEARCH...
WHO COULD BENEFIT FROM THIS SCRIPTURE?	I CAN VISUALIZE...
SYMBOLISM:	KEY EVENTS:

WHAT DOES GOD WANT ME TO KNOW?	HOW DOES THIS SCRIPTURE CONNECT TO MY LIFE?
IMPACTFUL VERSE:	KEY TAKEAWAYS:
IMPACTFUL VERSE:	KEY TAKEAWAYS:
IMPACTFUL VERSE:	KEY TAKEAWAYS:

Reading Log

Facts about Characters:	This scripture made me realize...
Impactful Words:	I need to research...
Who could benefit from this Scripture?	I can visualize...
Symbolism:	Key Events:

What does God want me to know?	How does this scripture connect to my life?
Impactful Verse:	Key Takeaways:
Impactful Verse:	Key Takeaways:
Impactful Verse:	Key Takeaways:

READING LOG

FACTS ABOUT CHARACTERS:	THIS SCRIPTURE MADE ME REALIZE…
IMPACTFUL WORDS:	I NEED TO RESEARCH…
WHO COULD BENEFIT FROM THIS SCRIPTURE?	I CAN VISUALIZE…
SYMBOLISM:	KEY EVENTS:

WHAT DOES GOD WANT ME TO KNOW?	HOW DOES THIS SCRIPTURE CONNECT TO MY LIFE?
IMPACTFUL VERSE:	KEY TAKEAWAYS:
IMPACTFUL VERSE:	KEY TAKEAWAYS:
IMPACTFUL VERSE:	KEY TAKEAWAYS:

About the Author

Christina DeMara is the idealistic creator of Early Life Leadership. Above that, she is a mother, wife, Christian, educator, author, public speaker, curriculum creative, and advocate for everything good in the world. Her first job, as a high school dropout at fifteen, was working for the Kirby Vacuum Company. She later completed her bachelor's degree in Interdisciplinary Studies with a minor in Special Education. She holds three master's degrees from the University of Texas—one in Special Education, one in Educational Administration and Leadership, and one in Curriculum and Instruction. She later studied business and leadership through Our Lady of the Lake University in San Antonio, Texas. She has experienced and studied extensively on leadership theory, organizational models, and business strategy. She is best known for her book Early Life Leadership in Children, and her interactive workbooks. Christina DeMara has overcome many obstacles in life through the grace of God. She enjoys spending time with her family, going to the beach, attending church, cooking, trying new restaurants, researching, teaching, and tackling do-it-yourself projects.

Christina has Facebook groups called:

I LOVE READING AND WRITING

&

I LOVE LEADERSHIP!

You are welcome to join!

LET'S STAY CONNECTED!

ChristinaDeMara@gmail.com

ChristinaDeMara.com

EarlyLifeLeadership.com

Follow Christina!
She would love to hear from you.

Your honest review is appreciated!

Thank you for reading!

CPSIA information can be obtained
at www.ICGtesting.com
Printed in the USA
FSHW01n1951040618
49053FS